100360 EN
Making a Space Shuttle

Lee, Mary
ATOS BL 3.5
Points: 0.5   LG

W9-AHA-756

Reading Essentials®
Exploring Science

Leveled content-area science books in Earth/Space Science, Life Science,
Math in Science, Physical Science, Science and Technology, and
Science as Inquiry for emergent, early, and fluent readers

Making a Space Shuttle
Written by Mary Lee

Text © by Perfection Learning® Corporation 2006

This Americanization of *Making a Space Shuttle* originally published in English in 2003
is published by arrangement with Oxford University Press.

Printed in China.

For information, contact

Perfection Learning® Corporation

1000 North Second Avenue, P.O. Box 500
Logan, Iowa 51546-0500.
Phone: 1-800-831-4190
Fax: 1-800-543-2745

perfectionlearning.com

PB ISBN 0-7891-6709-3
RLB ISBN 0-7569-6293-5

1 2 3 4 5 6   PP   11 10 09 08 07 06

Acknowledgements:

The Publisher would like to thank the following for permission to reproduce photograghs.
Getty Images - Photodisc p 5: Getty Images - Image Bank: p 9; Getty Images - Taxi: p 12

PERFECTION LEARNING®

Making a Space Shuttle

Mary Lee

Contents

Introduction 3

Space Shuttle. 6

   Orbiter 10

   Main Engine 11

   Fuel Tank 12

   Rocket Boosters 13

Making a Space Shuttle . . 14

Index 24

The planets in our Solar System

Introduction

For thousands of years people have looked up into the sky. They have looked at the moon and the Sun. They have looked at the stars. People always wanted to know what was in space, but they had no way of getting there.

spacecraft

rocket

Today, people can get into space. They can get there in spacecraft. The spacecraft have rockets fixed to them.

Have you seen fireworks on the Fourth of July? The rockets on spacecraft are like big fireworks. They burn and launch the spacecraft into the air.

This firework is a rocket.

Space Shuttle

A space shuttle carries astronauts into outer space.

Astronaut

One kind of spacecraft that you may know about is a space shuttle.

A space shuttle carries astronauts into space. A space shuttle uses rockets to launch it into space.

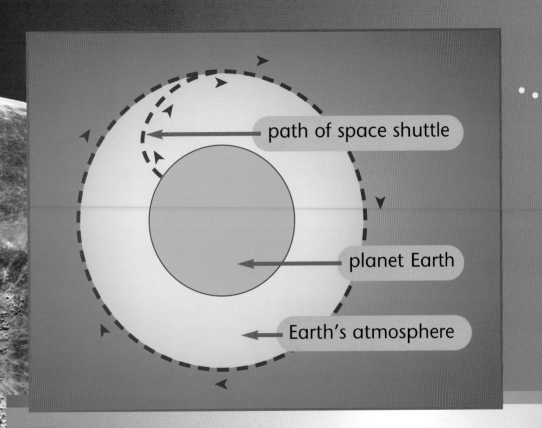

path of space shuttle

planet Earth

Earth's atmosphere

Rockets launch the space shuttle through
the Earth's atmosphere into space.
Would you like to learn more about
space shuttles?

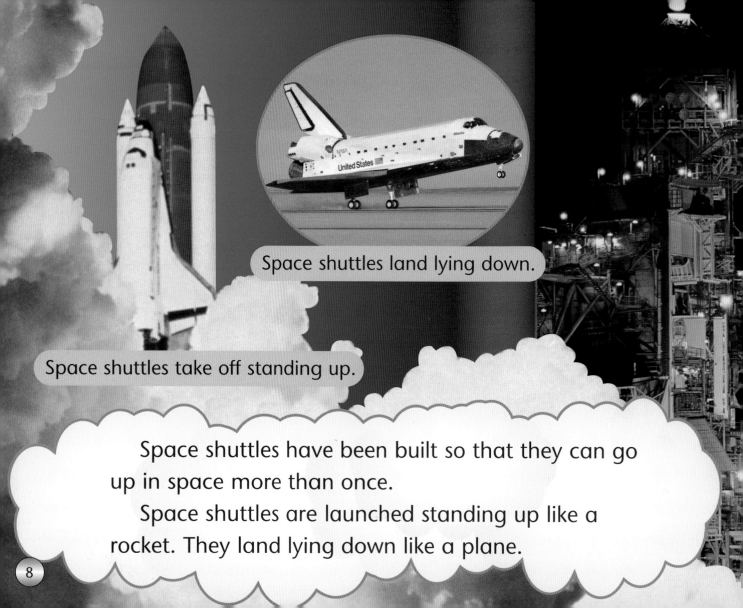

Space shuttles land lying down.

Space shuttles take off standing up.

Space shuttles have been built so that they can go up in space more than once.

Space shuttles are launched standing up like a rocket. They land lying down like a plane.

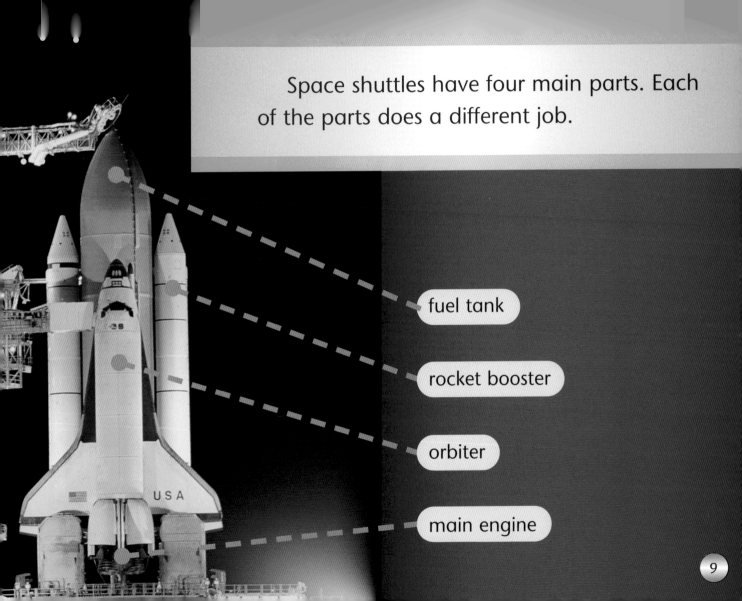

Space shuttles have four main parts. Each of the parts does a different job.

fuel tank

rocket booster

orbiter

main engine

Orbiter

The orbiter is the main part of a space shuttle. This is the part that travels around the Earth. The orbiter has a living room and a kitchen. The outside of the orbiter is covered with special tiles. The tiles stop the shuttle from burning up when it comes back to Earth.

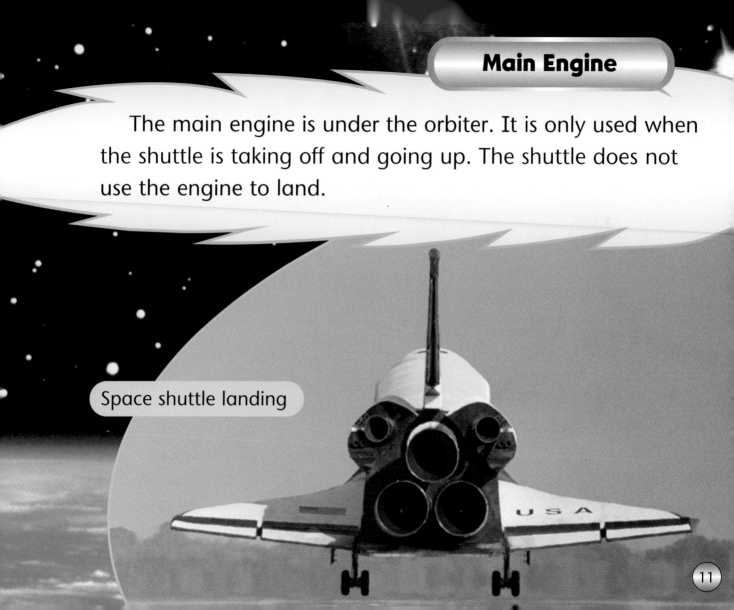

The main engine is under the orbiter. It is only used when the shuttle is taking off and going up. The shuttle does not use the engine to land.

Space shuttle landing

A space shuttle has a large tank of fuel for the engine. Like the engine, it is used when the space shuttle is taking off and going up. The fuel tank falls off when it is empty.

fuel tank

12

Rocket Boosters

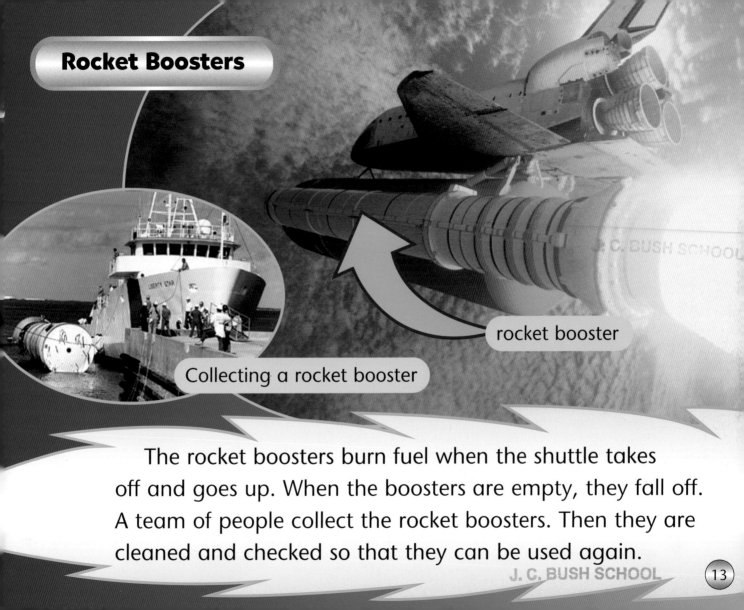

Collecting a rocket booster

rocket booster

The rocket boosters burn fuel when the shuttle takes off and goes up. When the boosters are empty, they fall off. A team of people collect the rocket boosters. Then they are cleaned and checked so that they can be used again.

Now that you know about space shuttles, you can make one.

You will need the following tools:

- scissors

- glue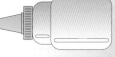

- sticky tape

- paint

- paintbrush

You will need the following materials:

- two cardboard circles

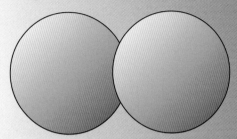

- one cardboard tube

- strong cardstock

Making the Space Shuttle

1. Use the cardstock. Cut out wing shapes.

2. Make two cuts at the bottom of the cardboard tube.

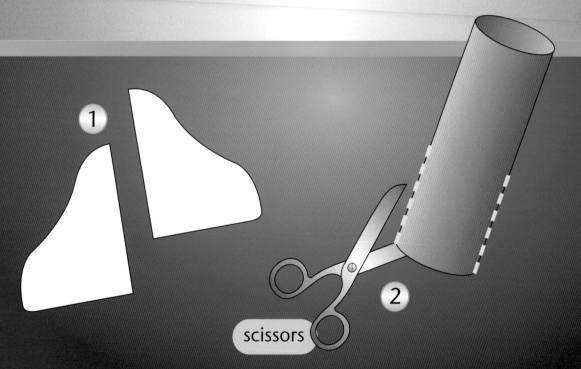

scissors

3. Slide the wings into the slits.

4. Attach them with sticky tape.

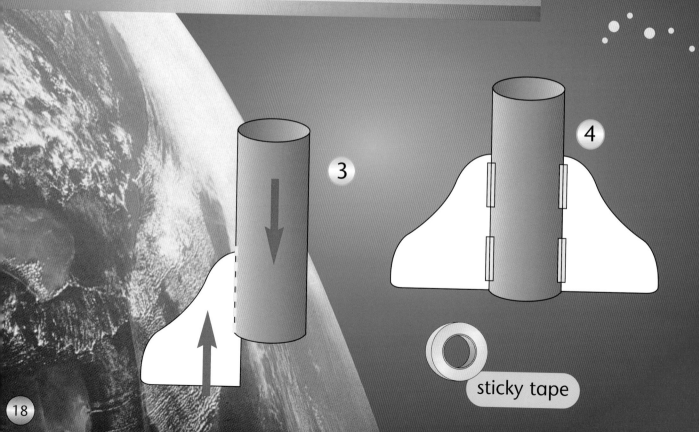

sticky tape

5. Make a cut in one of the cardboard circles.

6. Pull one side of the cut over the other side to make a cone shape.

7. Fasten it with sticky tape.

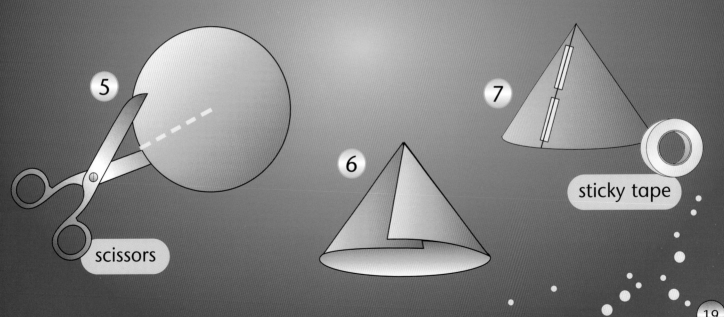

5

scissors

6

7

sticky tape

8. Put a cone shape in the bottom of the cardboard tube. Fasten it with sticky tape.

9. Put another cone shape on the top of the cardboard tube. Attach it with sticky tape.

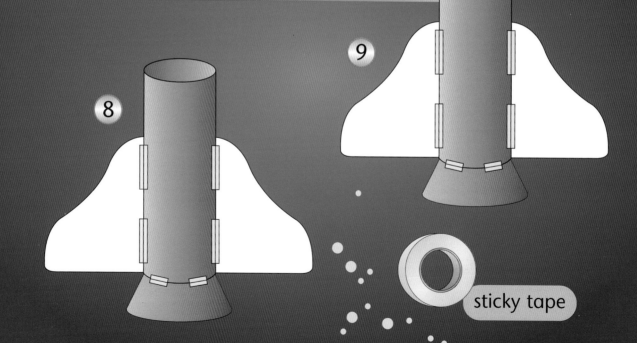

sticky tape

10. Cut lots of squares out of cardstock.
    These are the tiles for your shuttle.

11. Glue them onto the shuttle

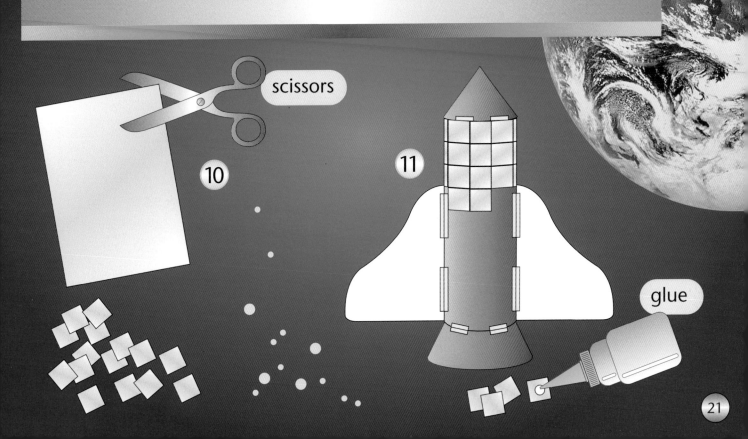

scissors

10

11

glue

12. Now, paint your space shuttle.

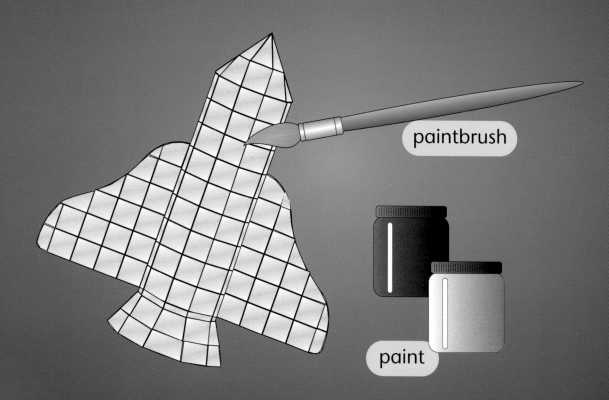

paintbrush

paint

This is your space shuttle.

Index

rockets, 4, 5, 6

space shuttles
model, 14–23
parts, 9–13